DATE DUE

Demco, Inc. 38-293

ENTERED JAN 1 2 2010

Other works by Ann Fisher-Wirth:

Poetry:

Blue Window

Five Terraces

The Trinket Poems

Walking Wu Wei's Scroll

Criticism:

William Carlos Williams and Autobiography:
The Woods of His Own Nature

CARTA MARINA

A POEM IN THREE PARTS

Ann Fisher-Wirth

WingsPress

San Antonio, Texas
2009

Cover image: From the *Carta marina et descriptio septemtrionalium terrarum* [Facsimile]. Malmö, AB Malmö, Ljustrycksanstalt, 1949. From the collection of the James Ford Bell Library, University of Minnesota. Used by permission. Interior map: "Carta Marina" (1539), engraved by A. Lafreri (1572). From the collection of the Uppsala University Library, Uppsala, Sweden. Used by permission.

First Edition

ISBN-13: 978-0-916727-56-7

Wings Press
627 E. Guenther
San Antonio, Texas 78210
Phone/fax: (210) 271-7805

On-line catalogue and ordering:
www.wingspress.com
All Wings Press titles are distributed to the trade by
Independent Publishers Group
www.ipgbook.com

Library of Congress Cataloging-in-Publication Data

Fisher-Wirth, Ann W.
  Carta marina : a poem in three parts / Ann Fisher-Wirth. -- 1st ed.
    p. cm.
  ISBN 978-0-916727-56-7 (alk. paper)
  I. Title.

PS3606.I79C37 2009
811'.6--dc22
                          2008039368

for Peter

There is no end of things in the heart.

The Carta Marina, "the earliest map to present a fairly accurate picture of Sweden and its neighbouring countries,"* was completed after twelve years' labor by the Swedish historian Olaus Magnus in 1539. Published in Venice, it was lost for many years. At present, two copies exist: one in the Hof- und Staatsbibliothek in Munich, and the other in the Carolina Rediviva, the Uppsala University Library. Made of nine woodcuts, the map measures 170 X 125 centimeters.

* *Commentary*, Uppsala Library, 1988

Contents

I.

Olaus Magnus' Carta Marina

I.

First,
>   notice
>   the bear,

a beer-belly bruiser
lounging on slabs of iceberg

with a salmon big as he is.

Ramming its tail between his legs,
he presses it like a lover,
wraps one arm around its neck, sinks his teeth

into its shoulder. North or to Heaven
the salmon stares while the other Ursa

Alba on a somewhat larger floe
snarls up at his rival's feet.

Ice broken off like a gingerbread house
piles to a peak in the Mare Glaciale;

though we are far far North,
here, alone of all the map, is iceberg.

Two swans sail in synchrony
above two eels or fish toward rocks where
a fiddler plays a tune

and a ferret or ermine runs home
to his mate peeking out from a shawl-shaped tunnel.

The fat-cheeked wind howls down from the West

on the tented plains
of Iceland.

II.

Marble that's gray as my clothes
gray as the rain gray as the streets gray as the Fyris river—

marble and water make patterns swirling into sleep
into featherbeds you seek, falling—

when you wake it's night when you walk it's night
when the sun slips through like a torn strip of primrose silk

behind the wet trees, the black and blotted October leaves
it's night again, nearly.

III.

Fragment: Email from Paris

Down they forgot as up they grew.
Unbeknownst, however, you have had no trouble

passing through my memory (remorse).
I was therefore happy to learn where you are.

If you were not living in Europe
I would probably not have written you now . . .

You, my first "real" girlfriend . . .

Peter's out walking in the forests—
           we're here in Sweden ten months, two gone already—

I sit on the floor in the dark exhibition room
                            of the Carolina,
and gaze through rainy hours at the wall-sized *Carta Marina*

Where like good little ponies, staunch soldiers,
        Olaus Magnus's identical
              woodcut trees
                  march along Frisia,
Saxonia, Holsathia, it is 1539,
        they make their stand
              in Samogethia, wind all the way north
                  through Russia Alba
where the wild boar
        charges and the chicken-creature
              runs screaming amok
                  toward the Muscovy king.

THE KEY TO THE MAP
(TRANSLATED THROUGHOUT BY PETER)

Pope Paul III   11 March 1539
In the Fifth Year of Our Pontificate

To the future memory of the matter.

Since as our beloved son Olaus Magnus
The Goth recently made known to us
That he himself wrote during a long time
And with great labor a geography
Or description of the Northern Places...

Olaus Magnus the Goth Salutations to His Kindly Reader

. . . This table of the Northern lands and of the marvels contained
in them (which I publish to the praise of the most serene Doge
Pietro Lando and of the Venetian Senate and to the public use of
the Christian world) is divided into nine parts according to the nine
major letters, ABC etcetera. ...Under what small letters the matter
that you seek is contained within a capital letter.

A   B   C   D   E   F   G   H   I

A

> The island of Iceland and its unusual miracles.

> > A

> > > Three mountains
> > > On whose exalted summits
> > > Is perpetual snow and in whose
> > > Bases eternal fire—

B

Four fountains, diverse in their nature.
By one, perpetual heat sent forth
Turns everything to stone
Remaining (however) in its proper form.
The second is intolerably cold.
The third flows with grain liquor
And the fourth exhales pestiferous contagion.

C

A fire pastures in water
And is not extinguished by it.

D

Ravens   white falcons
Picas   bears   foxes   white hares
Black foxes   also.

E

Miserable ice indicating faithfully
By the moaning of the human voice
That it causes the soul of a man
To be tormented there. . . .

———

Gnashing their teeth, the pig-faced
whales
furl spray
backward from spoutholes
that extend like gut or sausage
from their scalps. Their brows
furrow, their lower incisors
curl on their cheeks like scimitars

as a sailor
tootles loudly on the deck
and barrels bob in the pitching sea.

And jackdaws still
    scream and wheel
        in the Prussian blue sky.
            Ice on the rooftops.

                Head South now.

How can leaves hold so much light
while ice rimes every point of maple, of nettle—

Tonight, listening to that floating melody
at the heart of the Emperor Concerto,
listening to that single piano line rise softly

for a moment, like a stream wandering into
thin gold sky air
between thunderous cliffs of sound—

and that Chuck and Jonathan, my students, being newly dead
would never hear it, never sit in the Aula
gazing up at its leafy panels and painted dome of stars—

Fragment: Email to Paris

I am glad you told her you're writing me.
I don't want for there to be secrets.

To honor the present
and honor the past, be in the present

and not shut off the past—I think
it can be done, not lose the past, not lose

the thread of one's life, but allow it
to be transformed, so that loss

is not the whole story.
                    Yes, you were 19 and I was 18 . . .

I.

The woman stopped by the woods
        on the rocky path toward Sunnersta,
and knelt on the frosty
        ground in front of a birch tree.
It shook its leaves loose,
        golden leaves. She just
stayed there at the edge of it, white-haired, kneeling.

Yes, but this pain scares me.

II.

On the train to Eskilstuna—
                smudged-out land
                        bare fields
                dirty mist in the trees
(Peter is home again, walking all day)
                                pines in the distance
        only a few red leaves.
The fields are all harvested now   sharp
        stubble   red paint   that beautiful Italianate glow
                on the outbuildings
                        hay baled in white plastic.
And I'm going to Eskilstuna my chest killing me
        to talk to the future teachers about poetry.

—Want to sleep want a painkiller strong enough to take the pain
away so I can remember the suppleness of breathing   There's no
getting out of this easily   But schoolgirls in jackets their hair down
their back in braids chatter together happily   and it's 9:35 on the
train—

Red roofs this clayey red
                           as if someone remembered Mississippi

               as if someone remembered summer
                                 lemondrop yellow slatted wood
olive green   charcoal gray   the beautiful colors of houses
                                     and the lassitude
of willow trees reflected in the water.

—Oh something is all wrong in my back and the bones of my chest feel crushed   Is it my heart's hurt?   I draw breath like filling a glass up Narrow   Narrow—

In a crown of what seem daggers,
the demon sweeps his stables.
Ravenous, grinning, he brandishes a whisk broom.
Horses behind him whinny,
locked in their stalls, heads snapping.
From the stable door their piss runs,
river down mountains to the sea—

But wilder than Olaus Magnus' Norway,
the ultrasound,
bloody red screen
throbbing and pulsing in the middle of it,
and that is the fist of my heart,
knot tensing and then relaxing, red vortex,
nebula of my galaxy. I am so grateful to it
for pumping steadily, for not being too big,
I lie on my side and want to pat it. Nice heart.

B

It contains the first part of Greenland and its inhabitants
around the letter A

A

They show themselves to be expert sailors
Who shoot at ships

And they do this themselves safe
And from that the ships are turned over and sink—

But there's something, Peter says, he's just not getting.

B

Two very large sea monsters
        The one truculent with its teeth
                The other horrible with its horn.

                (Draped with spines and jewels
                like a fish-tailed warthog
                wearing a scalloped mantle

                And a tunafish wearing a clown hat)

C

An erect whale sinks a big ship
        With a look of dogged satisfaction....

H

A fisherman striking the ice with an ax
Stuns and captures the fish beneath.

I

Reindeer are domesticated in herds
And harnessed to chariots, surpass the fastest horses.

K

Demons serve themselves on the flesh of captured men.

L

A domesticated herd of reindeer moving according to
Custom on the frozen lake   toward
*   *   *minera auri*   gold mines.

Yes, but how do you map this sea, Olaus Magnus?

How do you carve these currents in your woodblocks?

Heart, you are gazing
at a girl
at the bottom of a well,
a girl in whose belly a child quickens,
who rises naked, calm
from her boyfriend's bed
and walks to the bathroom through dark
dark night, rosy calm girl
who sways a little, love-loosened, her breasts
warm on her belly, and you are gazing
at the smear of blood on the toilet paper,
then at her walking
back to the bed,
still naked,
and everything different forever then.

With that blood the girl,
oh her warm
body soft as a moth's wings
starts down its long
road toward November,
toward the forceps,
the stillbirth, the hospital bed—

And you are gazing
at a boy
who loves chess
and hates psychology, whose hands
are knob-knuckled
and eager and whose mouth

always tastes of Chesterfields,
a boy who keeps house with her
in his sister's house
when his sister is gone,
fog spilling across the Bay,
him buttering bread, reading the paper,
on the stereo Dylan
or Miles Davis,
them turning to the bed
like wind blows through eucalyptus trees
or rain runs down leaves
again, again—
a boy who will blame his body
that warm midnight and never
tell her, never
tell her why he vanished—

No, say it this way.

Playing house in 1965, the two of them drifted like leaves along
calm water, like air that eddies and flows first through her lungs,
then through his lungs, warmed by the heat of the stove, stirred by
the blades of the ceiling fan. And the child shifted and grew, an
elbow, a knee sculpting her side, its small life thrumming in her
bloodstream. For these few hours, spread over as many weeks, they
were a family.

After 37 years he has emailed. He's a doctor in Paris, he found me in
Sweden. "You drew back into yourself then," he writes, and though
I had forgotten, he's right. Between rising from the bed and coming
back to bed, I found the blood on the paper, and my heart chose. I
was spotting, I was terrified, I shut my body against him. And soon
the waters closed over us both.

So that now, come home tonight from the pub in downtown
Uppsala where I drank and grew desperate and hateful, and wanted
to write Peter a note that said simply, "Hurt me"—now how I want
to go back to that moment before the moment: that girl flushed,
rosy, the boyfriend at peace sprawled out long on the bed. She has
not started down the road yet toward the blood, the gray coffin. He
has not feared yet what he will fear for 37 years, and never spoke of
to a soul: that he murdered her child by fucking her.

I. The women of the Carta Marina

Her hair flows out behind her.
            Poised to shoot her arrow,
     she skis beside her lover
           in Finmarchia,
wearing Grecian robes
       and a white beret.

Two women worship a red cloth.
          Two are present
             for the pouring out of blood
     near the lion in Scricfinia.
These are pagans, given in marriage.

One leans against a grinning,
         three-antlered reindeer.

         Milk gushes
    into a wooden pail
from both udders, the one her hands press
       as well as the other. The woman
         is round-cheeked,
   sturdy. She gazes toward us.

Some of the bears and birds are girls.

      The sea's a girl, the map's a girl.

II. The Kingdom of the Animals

We watch them all, one mating act per meal.
It's the Discovery Channel, only
thing that's not in Swedish and not MTV.
He makes a leap, and the fried-egg edges
of her jump and twitch like water on a griddle.
This is stingrays, fleshy pancakes thrusting
and writhing; he holds her, the announcer says,
with one pod while the other pod acts like
a penis. When I was little I could never
say the word penis. By "little" I mean
under forty-five. And the gray shark bites her
pectoral fin and hangs on as over
and over they go, white bellies reaching,
roiling, nowhere joined yet except fin and teeth,
underwater Siva of a thousand flashing mirrors.

One night I stayed up late. I was lonely,
Peter was sleeping. A couple "made love"
in an MRI machine, barely able
to wriggle in the tube. I don't know
what the TV researcher wanted to determine,
but for days I held that image to my heart
like a hot water bottle, blurry length
of a cock tucked all the way up snug
to the mouth of a womb. They showed the cock
bends at the base to get in, like a strong
sapling. It snub-noses forward, like the
blind man I saw this morning, his white cane
feeling his way through a construction site.

There are states for which the body must seek images.
For instance, pain.

> If I lie very still, turning neither
> to the left
> nor to the right, this will pass.

> If I do not lift my head
> from the pillow, this will pass.

> A ship pulls into harbor—
> Bremerhaven, 1947—and, unloading cars,
> a car falls on a worker. I am a baby.
> He is crushed, his breastbone shatters.
> I remember shouts and swarming.

> Adam has taken his rib back and swallowed it.
> It travels inside his chest,
> as the hysterical womb
> used to wander the body of woman.
> It sharps, as Joshie said when he was three—
> one organ after another.

> If I do not turn in my stall, this will pass.

> "Learn to breathe into the side ribs,"
> the yoga teacher told me.
> "Learn to breathe into the belly,
> the back. That will keep your chest still."

The owl
glides on stealth wings at midnight
and once I saw it, heard it, rise
like a rocket over invisible fields,
the hare in its talons caught
in the headlights, still writhing.

Say yes to this, it will find its own shape.

Open.   Open.   Open.

Ungrateful wretch,
how can you fear me
who powers the leaf to green,
sends the magpie preening
after keys and baubles,
etches the crystal
in the melting snowflake?

The Swedish doctor said,
Be assured.
The pain is not your heart,
but in the cartilage and bone, the cage around the heart.

I. All Saints' Day

E

    Under A

       A

          Contains in this most ample region
              The Isles of Scandia
          From which once most powerful people went forth
              Into the universal orb.

       B

          Three crowns, arms of the Kingdom of Sweden.

       C

          A Lion armed, arms of the Kingdom of Norway.

       D

          A lake which is frozen with snow.

       E

          There from a cliff he seeks to know the depths of
          the inscrutable sea.

A man comes: *"Stängt. (Closed. Get lost.) Holy day."* He stands by
the library door till we leave.

    And dark walks down the street
        in its boots of wind or snow
            earlier and earlier and earlier . . .

II.

The doors stand ajar between the three realms.
The graveyard is a home of dancing lights today.

A few first snowflakes
wet the matted oakleaves, birchleaves,
and the candles are tongues of the dead.
Heimlich/unheimlich the ghostly ones flicker.
They turn to break a loaf or talk of ships,
to settle a quilt or braid a daughter's hair,
and the grave plots edged with stone and heather
are alcoves, rooms they live in.

We walk, holding each other close, through the luminous air
of a country not our country, where

They sit at scarred tables behind translucent curtains—

I.

You get to the point where everything becomes metaphor,
everything becomes signal.
Then you sicken.

The ship breaks apart and perishes, churns down the whirlpool
of your own obsessions—
                                    Yes, but
after the waters close
there is the vital sun,
and there are still whales there.

Sometimes they gaze back at you, calmly,
mother and baby still attached—

II.

—this about the boy & girl, not quite true.

It was late afternoon, not midnight,
on a daybed in an alcove by the kitchen.
Not true, he was the father of her child.
No, he was the boy she turned to.
Still, he covered her body
with the sweetness of warm rain.

Now snow comes down fast through lead-white skies
on the graves across the way
which are not graves, as I had fantasized, of seafarers, farmers,
but of men and women who turned to books—

Of Svante August Arrhenius
who predicted global warming,
Dag Hammarskjöld, his death

in an African plane crash one of the first
I remember, and Lotten von Kraemer, writer,
her beautiful face carved in profile
on her own—surprise—enormous headstone.

Of Erik Gustaf Geijer, whose students gave him the meadhorn,
and Gustaf Fröding, poet, crazy,
with the most candles of all, I counted them, nine—
who got into trouble for his notorious
poem, "A Morning Dream,"
which he called
to the end of his life "an exercise in purity,"

And of all the Carins and Folkes, Belias,
Jennys, Lennarts, Hjalmars, the babies
unbearably pitiful
buried outside the cemetery borders;

We listened to Verdi's "Requiem" at Uppsala Cathedral
and I realized, suddenly, *eis . . . eis . . .*
this music is praying not for *us*, the living, but for *them* . . .

Praying
grant them peace, Lord,
Chuck and Jonathan my students, grant
the babies, the babies in their gray coffins peace, Lord...

Snow furs the curved tiles
of the roof outside my window,
and snow licks the wall beneath the tiles
painted that Swedish red
like burning cheeks, like summer,

Like the future memory of the matter,
in this universal orb of *luft* and *eld* and *jord* and *vatten*.

The Carta Marina
of
Olaus Magnus

Olaus Magnus "Carta Marina" 1539
efter A. Lafreri, kopparstick 1572

II.

The Coming
of Winter

Friskis & Svettis the billboard blazed
as we passed the gym's murky windows
where crowds of Swedish legs
flung out in leg-lifts, and disco music

blared through frozen soccer fields.
Frisky and sweaty, likewise, the twenty little girls
who giggle over football-sized calzones

in Mama Mu, the restaurant the Turks run
with free milk for children, black and white
stuffed cows on a piano, where we've dropped in,
freezing, on our way back from the woods.

But in the booth facing me the twenty-first child
chews stolidly, gazing...
lost in whatever dream, as her duckling-colored

braids bob and her jaws revolve.
Above her pale blue jacket her eyes meet mine;
I look away, look back, she is watching me.
In this season of coming winter she is my daughter.

Angel with the stubborn underjaw,
fragile as snow,
persistent as dandelion roots,

she looks up at me
from lavender blankets tucked to her chin,
and my soul is weighed in her silence.

(Streaka / melankoli—

    the words I saw at random
           in the Swedish refrigerator poetry kit.

At Mama Mu I will have the streak of melancholy.)

———

    And in the woods, in Hågadalen Nåsten,
    we came to Rödmossen,
    "red mosses,"
    where the sun slanted across granite boulders;
    through bog, along boardwalks,
    we arrived where once I picked
    the last lingonberries
    that clustered like drops of blood in late September.
    As we stood in the new snow among scrub bushes,
    completely circled by birch trees,
    I thought: I wish we could die here,

    before I fuck it up—

while the sun slants into the cup of the clearing.

We walked in late September beneath the lindens
to Sunnersta where the lake opened out that first day,
dazzling. Two little girls, coltish, ten years old,

sat with their backs to us
on a rock they'd reached by climbing a plank

laid down from shore; they bent toward each other
giggling, murmuring, beneath willow leaves
that arched down, framing them. I have three girls,

two grown—   But how far away they are—
like those children in that season where the light

strobed between red apples   yellow apples
red apples on the trees   yellow apples on the ground
quick strobe back and forth, in the kingdom

of autumn. Now dawn breaks with a light
dusting of snow over the rooftops

of Uppsala. A crane, motionless,
its long arm horizontal above the buildings
like a ladder, is lit every few rungs,

all night the crane like a ladder of stars.
Heat pours out like sand in this apartment.

I have become one of those people
I swore I'd never be, shuffling duffers
in slippers, cold cream slathered

on my cracking skin, up at dawn to cope
with my arthritis. I gaze at myself

in the window as the sky now mottles,
slate, then a tenderer blue, and jackdaws
flying faster as the sun still, somewhere—

In the Gustavianum, the science museum,
there's an etching of a man, flayed.
His sad, bad face sags from one hand,
and the rest of his skin suit hangs like sleeper pajamas.
He's standing there wearing his muscles and blood veins.

—Correlative object for a wife
who's afraid she's falling in love
with another man,
with a lost man, a reappeared boy from her girlhood—
with the underside of a mirror, that icy mercury blackness

where the boy was her lover when her unborn daughter
swelled and rotted; what a mystery for the doctors,

what a mystery for the wife
who was this girl
who carries this child
forever, whose shadowy face is turned forever away from her.

My husband lets me on first, he's a gentleman,
but that means he's facing the mirror
as we ride up or down the five floors
to our apartment. Talking to me,
he watches himself until one day I say,
Stop looking at yourself all the time,
and then oh boy do I feel guilty
because who tell me who
hangs her face above the water, the

sleek black streaming hair
                    of the nearly frozen Fyris River
        that rushes, gleaming, past the waterworks, over the mill race.

⸻

The sun goes down at 3 p.m., and squabbling ducks play hockey
with the pucks of bread we feed them, skidding
on ice that tightens from the reedy shore
near Kung Carl Gustaf the pleasure boat. In September
we bought tickets to be tourists and
glide through dusk to Lake Mälaren.
We ate shrimp, toasted each other with wine
by the twilight window,
as parties of businessmen laughed and *skoaled*,
catching every single eye around their tables.
We wanted something more, even then—

⸻

                    Something more
like dark, like sleep, pouring through all the marrow of our bones;
we kept going up on deck, braced against the cold,
until a pearly cirrus strip
broke glimmering over the trees.
It couldn't be clouds for it was black, black night—

                              Oh yes,
they said on the pleasure boat,
                    it could be
                         you have seen the borealis.

One day the waters have their skin on.

The next day, after thirty-seven years,
a voice, a stone falls through.
And all the way down to the place
where currents cease
and the black light thickens, it enters you.

———

In love with me again—or, he says, still—
he sends me pictures of his family.
He's not that gawky boy anymore
who smoked Chesterfields, drove a Peugeot,
not the one I lay with on his sister's daybed.
He's at the beach in Birkenstocks and khakis,
an arm thrown round the shoulder
of one of his grinning blond sons,
who's now the age of that moody boy.
I remember the extra-long tibia, though, the wide
wide chest, the slab of hipbone. Oh the heart
wants it all, every lover forever in me,
every lick of the setting sun wetting the wintry birch trees.

The Anatomical Theater.
Six tiers, the steepest stairs I've ever seen,
with no benches, but standing room only,
climb the octagonal tower beneath the cupola
of the science museum, the Gustavianum.

We climb to the top, peer down. Our friend's
son, age eight, squeals with delight
when we tell him why it has to be freezing.

There's plenty of space for the crowd
who paid to gawk at the lozenge-shaped table.

Next door, the wall-sized reproduction
of "Pieter Pauw's Anatomy Lesson"
shows a similar space in Leiden. I sit on the floor
and study
      the whippet
            the hound
                  the child
the jostling and pointing burghers,

a knife, a gobbet of something, and tracings
of blood or leaves. The body's head flung back,
his sinewed arms, black feet. The doctor, kind eyes
and a bushy waxed mustache,
is mopping his wrist and holding his hipbone.
Three skulls form the base of the table.

Naturally, they're all men. Woman's down the hall;
her outstretched palm gestures
to the great leaved thing like a cabbage rose

that blossoms from her belly
with a baby curled inside. Beautiful words,
she's the *gravida kvinna* . . . But here
in the anatomical theatre are the black-robed ones,
the ones with doublets and swords,
the scholar, his glasses perched on his nose
and a huge banded volume before him.

And the wooden bucket.
      And the hound's dewlaps,
           the hound's maniacal eyes.

———

The criminal gutted beyond hope of heaven lies before them—
The head in profile is defiant: coarse black hair, wide mouth, broken nose.
A towel lapped over his shoulder as if carelessly laid down
after mopping up bile and blood, erases the edges of him,
flowing like muscle or sinew into the table.

What do they want to know, what do they hope for,
these grim, excitable, prosperous men,
hauling him from the firing squad, the gallows?
How the heart works, yes, or where may be found
the liver and spleen; the doctor's eyes
are kind and his hand nearly
loving on the hipbone, but the whippet
just wants blood. . . .
           Let be.

How hollow
      hollow is.
           The entrails gone.
             The ribcage soaring.

Snow coming down now, atomies of snow—

Dreams coming down now, atomies of dreams—

       The world
            is wide and full of wonders and as we fell,
  the sea rose up to meet us
            and the sun poured through the open window.
Having driven to the cliff, no matter how I tried to turn left
      the car turned
          right,
    no matter how I tried to back up the car
       inched straight ahead,
              and then over, over.
Get out of the car! I screamed to the children—
          then woke in a sweat, thinking,
    Oh God, I killed the kids—
              but as we fell,
   the dazzling sea rose up to meet
      the crimson Voyager, I knew I could live
through this free fall, could permit the sea to flood
   the open window—

My friend is there, in another dream, and she says to me,
"Here is something I brought you, from last summer."
She lets it fall open, she spreads it, an enormous
paper napkin printed with a photo she took last summer,
Peter and me naked in virulent color
sprawled on a beach, a sandy hillside, us scarlet,
cobalt, gold, electric—his beautiful burly torso, sharp knees,
cock lying soft against his thigh, beyond him my body naked,

us sloping gently flushed rosy and crimson, this was when I knew
we were married eternally, and I say "Yes, yes,"
to my friend, "that was a good vacation," while all the while
I'm thinking, *What have I done? What have I done?*

Vargtimmen—

the wolf hour, my friend on her farm tells me how the wolves
come back to Uppland, I imagine them hungry,

the bag of night draws tight as they approach,
as they converge
from every corner of the map, heads low, thick-ruffed necks stretched out,
the ragged silence
and their paws
soft on the earth, spit-glint on their teeth,
they sniff the quick
blood trace of hare, the piss of dachshund, poodle,

I wake every night at the wolf hour, the night, then night
grown yellow, electric with snow,

wake taut with him, shaken, of whom I do not, dare not, dream—

Red taillights lead me uphill, downhill—
I watch them from the bus's steamy window,

pressing my cheek against cold glass
as I'm carried from the airport past fields and factories,
past Märsta in the midnight

where the old men still hunt elk-moose
till bloody haunches fill their freezers.

It's not *this man* or *this man*, not
these golden daughters or *this dream-ravened swaddle:*
no, it's the doors closed or the doors opened,

it's the heart gone night. The gods
stream back and forth across the threshold.

You can ride it, you know,
get on the dark bus and let it carry you.
That's how I've always been, going home, going nowhere—

uphill, downhill, the taillights like rubies,
past fields where the trees are just darker effacings.

I know how to find you.
I go where your sleeping
is filled with the shadows
of leaves, where the leaves have
bled their green,
and all that remain are
their skeletons, nearly
transparent, translucent,
and tissue gone blurred as
the moon among clouds, as
the fur on a moth's wing,
and tips as if trailing
through water . . .

Such leaves are not common.
In this snowy country
they cherish them, save them,
the white *skelettbladen*—
like us, they have died, to
become more enduring.

They tell me that in the old times people
would light candles and just sit in the dark,
resting, being in the dark, and so I
have lit candles and though Uppsala spreads
around me and the Incan music weaves
up from the street where three men are playing,
collecting coins in a hat on the ground,
and though I hear the busses and sometimes
clanking, in what my husband once called this
soulless apartment, here is the shining
dark. We have not solved the problem of love,
have we? My small paper city
waves its banners and candlelight glints
and gleams on its red foil towers, its gold
and emerald windows, its silver domes
and star shield. The candles by the window
are flickering; on the table, calm
and seeking upward, they are like breath
that barely hovers at the threshold of the body.

———

Oh no, Horsey, we have not solved the problem of love.

> *Friend* is just a word.
> > *Love* is just a word.
> > > *In love* is just two words...

And if God is both infinitely far off, and everywhere,
        this corresponds to the two motions of the soul,
            toward hunger and toward plenitude—

My stillborn daughter's hair beneath my hand
fragile as snow,
and the hot, sweaty scalps of the boisterous children.

For the force behind the movement of time
is a mourning
that will not be comforted—

While sirens go by at 3 a.m., sawing the air
with their Swedish unhurried urgency,
and after the bars close, students
pour into the streets below,
shouting and chattering
and smoking too many cigarettes,
and my husband sleeps beside me,
beloved, actual,

You will gallop me to the edges of the map
and I will lie down there
to the ones that pass
like electrolysis
through and through the far fields of my body.

My tongue will cleave to the roof of my mouth
and my hands will burn and shake, lifting love
up from my belly,
up from my heart, throat, and away from me,
giving it
into the night air
as you, Horsey, graze peacefully on ice shards.

This is the last day of the gathering dark and I want it to go on
        forever.

It eats the sun that keeps me from my monsters.

Trucks start up in the dark. Advent lights,
those bulbed wooden trees, are shining in every window,
and the river, its savage braidings,
tightens and tightens, live still over the race, but sullen, whitening.
We're on countdown as sun smears blood at 3 p.m. on the horizon.
In the sacred grove of Gamla Uppsala—
the pagan burial mounds three miles outside the city—
what a howl must have gone up
from the furred starving ones, when nine of every creature
hung from the trees: males including kings, gutted.

I don't want solstice yet, don't want the bowl nearly brimming
with black
to tip toward light,
don't want the bushes to stand up tall
with their sticky buddings.

My teeth clamp shut to keep a fox from leaping from my throat.

      I want to fall and fall into a featherbed, a kicked twist of covers.

I want to suck this ragged fruit pit.

          My body is shivering like swampfire.

III.

Les Très Riches Heures

Olaus Magnus ends like me, says goodbye
again and again, there's always one more
word, one gesture, you think you've
said everything, think you can walk down the stairs
leaving the chocolate on the desk, the chameleon
in his cage, leaving the chestnut trees in blossom
and the cemetery walls far below you
with the graves of Heine, Stendhal,
La Goulue who invented the Can-Can,
leaving the room where you gazed on the rooftops
of Paris, sleepless, unable to sleep,
night after night from the eighth story window—
think you can pick up your suitcases, bless
the house, bless the air in the house
and the fading lilies, the kitchen dishtowel,
and close the door behind you, enter April—

———

Here's Olaus Magnus:

In addition, Dearest Reader,
lest you run into difficulties in this brief index,
consult the future books in which one summary of the whole map,
with the miraculous things of the North,
will be declared.
Farewell.

They are sold at the Apothecary Thomas de Rubis
at the sign above the bank
near the Bridge of the Rialto
in Venice.

———

And here's the season:

Fragment: Emails from Paris

> *We need to see each other.*
> *Why not come in April and visit us?*
>
> *Peter, my wife, we can be friends,*
>   *we all need to meet—*

I.

On Slottsbacken, Castle Hill,
          we thirty stand in vigil
                   beneath a statue of Gunnar Wennerberg,
       whose *Gluntarne*, or "Big Boys," praised drinking
and student life at Uppsala.
                       Cold stone,
     his frock coat and silly flowing hair,
his slender arm cocked high above the Queen's Road.
                The castle's towers rise
         through branches leafless still,
behind faces like petals,
       brows and cheeks shadowed here
and here above clear cupped votives, white candles.

Gonna lay down my sword and shield—
             How to stop it, how to make the warmongers stop,
      make them back off, all winter we marched,
            millions marched—
                 and in Stockholm soldiers with guns
guarded the American Embassy—

            Tonight
it's nearly spring.
          Somewhere green begins again.
     The votives,
              seeds or beads of fire,
will burn all night when we have gone,
                and jackdaws soar at dawn
     around the spires of the cathedral.

II.

I saw her photo, Rachel Corrie,
a daughter not much younger
than my daughters,
legs broken, blood pouring
from her nose, her friends
in shock holding her.
Crying over the keyboard,
I phoned Peter. We walked
in the Stadsskogen, unruffled
Uppsala, watching the magpies
mass sticks and twigs
high in the trees like squirrels' nests,
beehive hairdos, wads of mistletoe—
the gleaming birds
meaning to have spring again.

This dance of the failing body parts
between us, who have found each other
again, who blossom if only by
email, after thirty-seven years—
He emails from the hospital:
lay down to read a book I recommended,
suddenly coughed blood,
finished the book in the ECU.
I write him the saga of my busted
ski knee—no sooner tried to turn than I
was moaning in the snow, remembering,
too late, I have faulty ligaments.
He tells me he did yoga, meditated
for years, till they found the scoliosis.
I describe my broken molar, the joints
or pulled muscles that make the heart cage ache,
make sleeping a matter of pills and prayer.
—This awkward, scary love, the way
snow falls everywhere, the way rivers
leap their banks in spring, and sunlight warms us.

He and I will rarely see each other, never
sleep together. So what do we write about;
what do we find to say, what cadences,
croonings of vowels, consonantal clicks and burrs;
labials for lips on the back or cheek,
for bread crumbs scattered on a kitchen
counter; verbal entanglings instead of
flushed limbs sprawled in the sunlight, candlelight?
Oh, work, war, children, or the carmine stucco,
the mottled, rippling roof outside my window.

Will these suffice us, will these sustain us
into age and death, these emails?

He writes back, "It's too easy,
turning bodies into words." Yes,
too easy—but tell me, what would *you* do?

Funny how memory misremembers.

I thought, Well of course I love this man,
we had a child together.

Now, the sweetness of the dead baby, her power
to carve channels of suffering and dream
in the soul like a mighty river—

                 And lying in bed
this morning as mourning doves
and small chittering birds fill the air,
I remember those months I lived
at the Florence Crittenden Home,
the girls who kept their babies, the girls
who gave them up—

Especially one, who reached her arms out
for her daughter, unwrapped her, kissed her fingers,
caressed her body, wrapped her,
cupped her one last time against her shoulder

(sick for my dead baby I was trying not to watch)—

gave her to the nurse who stood there waiting.

Can't sleep.

Looking out the window I see
Montmartre, where my mother bought the painting
one rainy Sunday when I was nineteen.
She carried it home through the rain,
a painting of buildings, rough black brushstrokes—
forty years later
it was still on the top shelf of the guest room closet—

———

Want to go down and wake him up,
talk to him.

You. You.
Why did you go out of my life thirty-seven years ago?

So all the rest could happen, your children, your great love.
So, in my zany way, at the ninth or tenth or eleventh hour
I could come galumphing up the hill again.

And my lost baby was here tonight
when we saw each other again,
we who loved when she was the fidget, the freight,
the sweet curled countershove
where you nested high in my body.
We drank whiskey, wine,
me with Peter, you with your wife. You sat across the room from me.

Are you looking at me are you looking at him
            are you looking at him looking at me

I am looking at you I am
                looking at you looking I am
glancing at your glance
            over crudités and pain
                    over omelettes aux fines herbes
pouring a glass of wine   I am watching you
                watch me as I glance
away I am watching you watch him   watching
            you glance at him raising
                    a napkin to your lips   glance
                        at him loving
his face   his big old backspringing fingers
            glance at him shaking
                    the salt on your food
watching the watcher who watches you

When I was young, Yeats said, I wanted to take off my clothes,
                        now I want to take off my body.

            Or lie down together—
    ah, but how?
            for I love my husband
                    for his wife is not my enemy

            All of us lie down together

    Ha!

All of us lie down together
    Flop
        Sprawl on the sidewalk in Seine *Savasana*

Take me   take me   take me   river

April 5. Afternoon

Marc Chagall, "Pâques"

Red wine
                         Green wings in a
            charred world
                    The angel of death
                                passing over

You cup a blossom in your hands,
and it becomes love's effigy:
all that you would give: carry it
to the altar of the heart,
which is black in a crimson room,
though here the spider makes lace
and the chameleon waits, all night if need be,
pulsed thing gentle till the viscous tongue
darts out to catch the cricket. Crunch,
its filamentous legs splay sideways
from the chameleon's mouth, then vanish,
gulp, and once again all's quiet in the velvet
emerald belly. You cup a blossom
in your hands, magnolia, its petals
like the silky white insides of thighs;
or maybe you bury your face in the pollen
of lilies. Whichever, it's all one.
You do not get to choose, beyond a simple
yes or no. Heine's buried next door,
who asked, *"Sagt mir, Was bedeutet der Mensch?"*
And Stendhal, who wrote *On Love.*

Finally, the world is irrelevant.
All that counts is what remains in your heart.
And the chestnut trees around you,
each with its thousand candles.

But that's not true, is it:
"All that counts . . ."

The nameless singing bird in Paris
slices the hour before dawn into crust and crumb.
His silver knives cut also
the peel from the orange, the notched
rooflines of houses. I'm in the living room,
sleepless, this
is ridiculous, I cannot, cannot—

And the cloth will lie bare on the table
when the sleepers waken
to the tidy day.

The solitary, singing bird in Paris—

Sous le pont Mirabeau
coule la Seine, Peter knows all the words

to all the poems, and we walked,
my arm in his,

along the midnight Seine
with its thousand flashing knives and mirrors.

Now the green and yellow cloth on the nail,
the white kitchen stool, the loud clock ticking—

Solitary bird in Paris
the scrabble and purchase and lilt of your song
carries me toward   *fare well*   toward   *God be with you*

Bird who sings before dawn over the rooftops the lilacs
just blooming
how can we stand to say good-bye
to the ones we love

And the clock ticks
and the lilacs, their shattering beauty
intensifies daily

Every night I wake at the wolf hour,
Vargtimmen, the hour when men go mad,
the hour of dread, despair,
of suicides and births. Last night
when I woke I asked it, What do you want
from me? What do you need from me?
And saw this: black   black   until a line
across created a horizon.
Then bulge, an arc of light,
as if a moon were rising. The arc
of light became a fold in darkness,
and from it, one by one, great wolves
ran toward me. They did not
mean me harm. They were the forms
that flow from pure dark's pure light.

I said to Peter, "Now I will turn the wheel
and finish the cycle with spring poems,"
and he answered—not mean, amused—

"What a new idea." So here it is snowing in Växjö,
flaking from a thick gray sky
on the buildings' ugly shoulders.

I stink of desire.
All I know is, I will either go or stay.
I carry the medlar of my own corruption.

My leg across Peter's belly,
I said, "I love you both," and he smiled,
held me. He said, "I love what is real."

We lay in our bed
remembering Chagall, the man and woman floating
radiant, newlywed, forever above the city,

the barn roof decorated with a shadowy third eye
above a green village,

the white cow looking up
with gentle eyes, *La Guerre,*
and the flames of all the world,
people fleeing, their wagons and carts,
the cow like a wave of torment and gentleness.

April was those paintings
and the war
and the windy light in Paris, April
was the man's spine, his whole torso,
trembling violently, his arms around me,
we sat on the bench where he goes to think
and he shook until the cold sun calmed him.

The branch outside my window
                        shakes with light.
Laughing gulls with sleek black heads
scream, it's springtime near the Fågelsång Café.
Babies in strollers squint into the wind
at a toddler under a thick plaid coat
who swaggers down the street in Batman sunglasses.
Look at the feathers, for Easter—magenta,
lime green, yellow, orange, in buckets
on corners, chicken feathers blazing,
glued to willow wands.

The year fattens. Seeds, seeds
riot in the ground. Daffodils swell.
Here, and here, though trees are leafless still,
gold breaks out in scribble of forsythia.

text

(Olaus Magnus, still
trying to end the *Carta Marina:*
on the far right side in Russia Alba,
a weasel in an ice cave, looking backward,
holds up a sign or scroll that says):

Olaus the Goth, to the kind Reader:

Because, Dearest Reader, the Scandinavian Isle,
according to Pliny the Elder in his *Orb of the Earth*
and Jordanes the Goth and Paul II,
is called the Vagina or Womb of peoples,
and by many writers is considered the King of States,
I have thought it worthwhile to indicate
the names of some of the people who went forth
from there on the page below.
                              Farewell.

(A shape like a womb
with, written on it: From Scandinavia
and then   Norway   Gothia   Sweden
and branches from this organ:)

Goths	Swedes	Danes	Northmen
Ostragoths	Lombards	Dacians	Picts
Visigoths	the Turkish Tongues	Slavs	Carpi
Gepides	Avars	Rugi	Caibi
Samogetes	Heruli	Alani	Cimmerians
Massogetes	Vinuli	Burgundians	Cimbrians
Huns	Swabians	Sembi	Bulgarians
Amazons	Swoss	Livoni	
Parthians	Tahidhali	Sciri	

                    And a lion
              In the far right corner:
          Behold the terrible lion
          Whom a mouse freed from his
          Bands thus the great are often
          Helped by the smallest labor.

          CONQUER EVIL WITH GOOD

                   ———

Farewellfarewellfarewellfarewellfarewellfarewellfarewell
    or as Prospero says in Swedish, *Var frei*. Be free.
                  Farvel.

Only a few weeks left.
                    I am starting to say

Good-bye to Kung Krål, anniversary restaurant
where we ate steak dripping with bloody juices
and slathered in béarnaise, and cress and oyster
mushrooms, and the best fries in Sweden

Goodbye to yellow finches, to laughing gulls
that throng the park near the Fågelsång Café,
to jackdaws in peppery clouds around the Domkyrkan,
huge messy magpie nests, and magpies prancing,
their bottlegreen sheen and preen

Goodbye to the Pumphuset where in spring
rushes the thawing Fyris River

And Santorini on the river, goodbye
to its moussaka, souvlaki, the waitress
six feet tall with towering hair and skintight clothes,
goodbye to her sloe eyes, her slink and grin, the icy glasses of retsina

Goodbye to Swedish Throwing Up Sickness,
that's what they really call it, that I got after eating moussaka,
and Peter held my head all night,
goodbye to five days of weakness and misery

Goodbye to the cobblestones, the pavingstones,
goodbye *slut spurt* our first Swedish words,
tillbaka and *tack så mycket,*
ursäkta, varsågod,
svartsjuk, bitterljuva,
and my favorites, *svamp* and *kyckling*

Goodbye to our bed with its featherbed,
and to making love to the cries of seagulls

Goodbye to the Swedish sun after endless gray,
and the students singing each Saturday night
in the streets below our apartment,
and the happy shouts and crashing bottles

———

And goodbye
to the most beautiful roof in the world—

old terra cotta scalloped tiles
light-kissed, with wavy striations of shadow,
and channels of shadow vertically,

bare trunk and branches of a linden tree
cutting up across the corner of the roof,
a pattern of shadows flung

down across the roof, and a little
black ventilation pipe sticking up partway along.

This is the roof I have gazed at all year
out my office window, while writing him,
through snow and gray and now brilliant blue.

Now light.

Lichens and dirt add another layer, of smudge
and blur and time. A roughness, a texture. A patina.

There was a day—three days—
I would have gone with him.

                    What does it matter?

As my Hindu friend said long ago
about something else entirely,

                    It's just emotions.

At Rödmossen

        little balls of deer dung   broken
pinecones   lingonberry leaves
winter-dried   sphagnum-covered   crimson-tipped mosses
        the year's first ladybug
each ant in the ant mound   frenzied   scurrying

            the faint twee-ip of a faroff bird

my husband's hair   shaggy   silver
as he lies sleeping on the moss
his tin and reindeer Lapp bracelet
fiery   like diamonds.

Light

                    light

saturating this bowl
of cedar- and birch-ringed bogland.

Promiscuous   indiscriminate   without reck or care
                    it pours on the yellow butterfly

the duff of pine needles
the gnarled, back-twisted cedar branch—

The split heart—

                              The heart still split—

All this human love and anguish—

Notes

Olaus Magnus' *Carta Marina*

"The doors stand ajar between the three realms": At the beginning of winter, according to ancient festivals, the doors between heaven, earth, and the underworld open. Christianized, this is the time of All Saints' Day (Hallowe'en) and All Souls' Day (November 1).

luft	air
eld	fire
jord	earth
vatten	water

The Coming of Winter

The Anatomical Theater: Olof Rudbeck (1630-1702), a naturalist, medical scientist, historian, and antiquarian, was a luminary of Uppsala University, where he taught for many years. "Pieter Pauw's Anatomy Lesson" is an engraving by Andreas Stock after a drawing by Jacques de Gheyn, Amsterdam, 1615. The picture of the pregnant woman is from Spigelius, "Opera," 1645. By law, only executed criminals were dissected.

The "skeleton leaves" are, I believe, linden leaves.

"The force behind the movement of time is a mourning that will not be comforted" is quoted from Marilynne Robinson's novel *Housekeeping*.

Gamla Uppsala, "Old Uppsala," is the oldest pagan site in Europe. It is written that sacrifices took place there every nine years: nine males of every creature, including humans, were killed and hung in a sacred grove. Gamla Uppsala contains important burial mounds and is the site, as well, of the original cathedral.

Les Très Riches Heures

The 23-year-old American student Rachel Corrie was bulldozed to death on March 16, 2003, while peaceably protesting the destruction of Palestinian homes on the Gaza Strip.

"Sagt mir, Was bedeutet der Mensch?" –"Tell me, what does a human being mean?"

"Finally, the world is irrelevant. All that counts is what remains in your heart" is quoted from Sándor Márai's novel *Embers*.

"Sous le pont Mirabeau coule la Seine" is the first line of Guillaume Apollinaire's poem "Le Pont Mirabeau."

In 1967 Ingmar Bergman's film "Vargtimmen" or "Hour of the Wolf" was released. The lines "The hour when men go mad, / the hour of dread, despair, of suicides and births" paraphrase a passage by Bergman that has been used to introduce the film.

slut spurt	greatly reduced, as in a final sale: final spurt
tillbaka	back (as in, money back)
tack så mycket	thanks so much
ursäkta	excuse me
varsågod	you're welcome: be so good
svartsjuk	jealous: black-sick
bitterljuva	bittersweet: bitter-lovely
svamp	mushroom
kyckling	chicken

Acknowledgments

I **am grateful** to the Fulbright Commission and to Uppsala University, Sweden, for awarding me the 2002-2003 Fulbright Distinguished Chair in American Studies, and to the members of SINAS and the English Department in Uppsala for their welcome and hospitality. And also to the University of Mississippi for awarding me a sabatical, which permitted me to spend the year in Sweden.

Thanks to Jessica Fisher, whose words got me started: "Write poems about the *Carta Marina*." Thanks to Beth Ann Fennelly, Pat Fargnoli, and Liz Kella. Thanks also to Pamela Uschuk, who led me to Wings Press, and to my editor, Bryce Milligan.

Thanks to Allan Hance.

And first, last, and always, thanks to Peter Wirth.

I am indebted to the following publications for their support of my work as this poem evolved:

An earlier version of Part I, under the title "Olaus Magnus, Carta Marina," won a 2003 Malahat Review Long Poem prize and is published in *The Malahat Review*.

An earlier version of the poem no longer titled "The Anatomical Theatre" appeared online in *Poetry Daily*.

The poem no longer titled "The Skeleton Leaves" appeared in *Metrical Salt*.

An earlier version of the poem no longer titled "There Ought to Be a Poem" ("This dance of the failing body parts between us") appeared online as part of the chapbook *Walking Wu Wei's Scroll* in *The Drunken Boat*.

About the Author

Ann Fisher-Wirth is the author of two books of poems: *Blue Window* (Archer Books, 2003) and *Five Terraces* (Wind Publications, 2005). She has also published two chapbooks: *The Trinket Poems* (Wind, 2003) and *Walking Wu Wei's Scroll* (online, *The Drunken Boat*, 2005). Her awards include a *Malahat Review* Long Poem Prize, the Rita Dove Poetry Award, a Poetry Award from the Mississippi Institute of Arts and Letters, and two Poetry Fellowships from the Mississippi Arts Commission. She has received six Pushcart nominations and a 2007 Pushcart Special Mention.

She has held a Fulbright lecturership at the University of Fribourg, Switzerland, and the Fulbright Distinguished Chair in American Studies at Uppsala University, Sweden. She teaches English and Environmental Studies at the University of Mississippi. She and her husband have five grown children.